PRACTICING THE PRESENCE OF THE LIVING GOD

A Retreat with Brother Lawrence of the Resurrection

PRACTICING THE PRESENCE OF THE LIVING GOD

A Retreat with Brother Lawrence
of the Resurrection

Jean Maalouf

ICS Publications
Institute of Carmelite Studies
Washington, DC
2011

The Scripture quotations contained herein are from the New Revised Standard Version Bible.

Practicing the Presence of the Living God quotations contained herein are from The Practice of the Presence of God by Brother Lawrence of the Resurrection, Critical Edition by Conrad De Meester, OCD, Translated by Salvatore Sciurba, OCD, with a Foreword to the American Edition by Gerald G. May, M.D., (Washington, D.C.: ICS Publications–Institute of Carmelite Studies–1994). Abbreviation used here: Presence.

Library of Congress Cataloging-in-Publication Data
Maalouf, Jean.
  Practicing the presence of the living God : a retreat with Brother Lawrence of the Resurrection / by Jean Maalouf.
      p. cm.
    ISBN 978-0-935216-77-6
    1. Lawrence, of the Resurrection, Brother, 1611–1691. Pratique de la présence de Dieu.
    2. Spiritual life—Catholic Church. I. Title.
    BX2350.3.M24 2010
    248.4'82—dc22
                                        2009054270

The holiest, most ordinary, and most necessary practice of the spiritual life is that of the presence of God. It is to take delight in and become accustomed to his divine company, speaking humbly, and conversing lovingly with him all the time, at every moment, without rule or measure, especially in times of temptation, suffering, aridity, weariness, even infidelity and sin.

—*Presence*, 36

Everything is possible for one who believes, still more for one who hopes, even more for one who loves, and most of all for one who practices and perseveres in these three virtues.

—*Presence*, 35

Also by Dr. Jean Maalouf

Bold Prayers from the Heart

The Divine Milieu: A Spiritual Classic for Today and Tomorrow (Essay)

Experiencing Jesus with Mother Teresa

The Healing Power of Faith

The Healing Power of Forgiveness

The Healing Power of Friendship

The Healing Power of Hope

The Healing Power of Joy

The Healing Power of Kindness

The Healing Power of Love

The Healing Power of Peace

The Healing Power of Prayer

The Healing Power of Purpose

I Can Tell God Anything: Living Prayer

Intimacies: The Miracle of Love

I've Got One Life to Live: Radiant Health God's Way

Jesus Laughed and Other Reflections on Being Human

Mother Teresa: Essential Writings (Editor)

In memory of my parents and teachers
who taught me so much
about the practice of the presence of God
and shaped my values.

Contents

Introduction

Today we live in a time and world of paradoxical blessings. On the one hand, we are witnessing the extraordinary scientific and technological progress that can facilitate an easier, less burdensome life on earth, while on the other hand we are confronted with the often-unexpected results of such rapid progress. While we can easily communicate through our wireless devices and the Internet, we seem to have lost the subtle touch of heart in our communications. Today we can enjoy more opportunities for reaching our goals in life, and yet the deepest, most meaningful purpose of life seems to be just beyond our grasp.

As a result, we often feel vulnerable, and to distract ourselves from our most profound needs, we buy into the culture of consumerism and instant gratification. We turn to external rewards and the short-term euphoria of new experiences, new relationships, new "things" (homes, cars, clothes, etc.), new solace through drugs and alcohol—anything that fulfills us as people who are living "in a hurry" without the time to slow down. We live with highs and lows, thinking that this is the way life is supposed to be.

Situations of loneliness, stress, restlessness, brokenness, depression, violence, injustice, poverty, and fascination with the superficial in today's world are numerous and tragic. It is important to understand them by seeking their structural causes and extirpate their deep roots, which can be found in the very quality of the human-divine relationship. Indeed, it

1

would be infinitely unhealthy and uncomfortable not to be able to narrow the gap that exists between us, and especially between us and God. Connectedness, not alienation; unity, not fragmentation; communion, not separation, is the answer to our lonely individual lives as well as to our stressful modern life. Thus, the importance of practicing the presence of God as a way of life seems crucial. One does not heal an illness by treating the symptoms, nor can one solve a problem without digging to the root causes of that problem. The remedy and the solution are found at a much deeper level.

A very helpful and inspiring guide on this path is a little book called *The Practice of the Presence of God*, written by the lay Carmelite Brother Lawrence of the Resurrection.

The Practice of the Presence of God

The Practice of the Presence of God is a little book that can be read in about two hours yet its content encompasses a lifelong application that is life changing. Its message is transformative in its utmost clarity and simplicity because it reveals the heart and soul of everyone's life purpose and work—to live joyfully in the presence of God, no matter what our circumstances are.

In this little book, Brother Lawrence reveals a very ordinary life that most of us would not really desire, and yet as he fulfilled his everyday duties in the midst of the most mundane and tedious tasks, he learned to live the happiest and most rewarding life. With his gracious humility, "he thought . . . only of doing little things for the love of God, since he was not capable of doing great things" (*Presence*, 94). Indeed, he modeled a life lived in the glory of God's love, peace, and joy.

No wonder this book was called a "little spiritual classic," a "devotional masterpiece," an "unparalleled classic," and is "relevant and timeless." For Dorothy Day, "It is a classic, and carries a message, points a way. It tells of spirituality which is within the reach of all." John J. Delaney says in the introduction of his own translation of this book: "[This book] has in common with all literary works of lasting value and timelessness that makes it as relevant and rewarding today as it was three hundred years ago; and I daresay it will be just so relevant and rewarding three centuries from now." Pastor A. W. Tozer wrote: "One of the purest souls ever to live on this fallen planet was Nicholas Herman, known as Brother Lawrence. He wrote very little, but what he wrote has seemed to several generations of Christians to be so rare and so beautiful as to deserve a place near the top among the world's great books of devotion. The writings of Brother Lawrence are the ultimate in simplicity; ideas woven like costly threads to make a pattern of great beauty. . . . Brother Lawrence is well established in the affection of spiritual souls of all denominations and every shade of Christian thought."

> This book was called a "little spiritual classic," a "devotional masterpiece," an "unparalleled classic," and is "relevant and timeless."

Furthermore, it is also no wonder that this book has been reprinted again and again, translated into many languages, praised by Catholics and non-Catholics alike, and largely circulated throughout the world. It seems that the ever-widening impact of this book appears to have been predicted by its own words, "When God finds a soul penetrated by an intense faith he pours out his graces in abundance. This torrent of his grace, impeded from running its ordinary course, expands impetuously and abundantly once it has found an outlet" (*Presence*, 50).

The Practice of the Presence of God is simply a collection of documented conversations, letters, and spiritual maxims that reveal the heart of a humble man and his intimacy with God. Perhaps a few lines from the twelfth letter will explain what this man is trying to convey to us:

> In several books I found different methods to approach God and various practices of the spiritual life that I feared would burden my mind rather than facilitate what I wanted and what I sought, namely, a means of being completely disposed to God. This led me to resolve to give all for all. Thus, after offering myself entirely to God in atonement for my sins, I renounced for the sake of his love everything other than God, and I began to live as if only he and I existed in the world. Sometimes I considered myself before him as a miserable criminal at his judge's feet, and at other times I regarded him in my heart as my Father, as my God. I adored him there as often as I could, keeping my mind in his holy presence, and recalling him as many times as I was distracted. I had some trouble doing this exercise, but continued in spite of all the difficulties I encountered, without getting disturbed or anxious when I was involuntarily distracted. I was as faithful to this practice during my activities as I was during my periods of mental prayer, for at every moment, all the time, in the most intense periods of my work I banished and rid from my mind everything that was capable of taking the thought of God away from me. (*Presence*, 75)

The Practice of the Presence of God has sometimes been referred to as the "methodless method" to living in God's constant presence. Yes and no. Yes because we cannot find here a logical and precise system that leads us step by step toward God—there is no structured method to follow. Yet there is no better and more efficient method than turning over to God our whole heart and will and allow God to work in us and through us. Only then we begin to see as God sees, think as God thinks, and act as God acts.

The reader of *The Practice of the Presence of God* cannot fail to notice Brother Lawrence's freedom from dogmatism while he espouses orthodox theology with childlike simplicity. Faith is expressed through the pages of the book as a living experience, rooted in the actual grace of God, and tested in the reality of everyday life.

Every word in the book radiates the living presence of God, and readers will find their hearts transformed by the Christlike humility gradually enveloping their minds and souls. Like St. Francis of Assisi who said more than eight hundred years ago, "Preach the word of God wherever you go, even use words, if necessary," Brother Lawrence lived the word of God every day in his actions and his "words."

The Practice of the Presence of God is a book of integration—faith and trust, life and prayer, contemplation and action, spiritual and temporal, and sacred and mundane. God wants to be present in every area of our life every second, twenty-four hours a day, and seven days a week. Prayer, then, would appear to have three essential elements: God, the person who is praying, and the relationship between God and that person. This is why, when we have a loving relationship with God, we are all the time in a state of prayer—unceasing prayer.

The reader of *The Practice of the Presence of God* will also notice how simple this book is; it is extraordinarily ordinary and common. There is no literary pretense at all here, no sophisticated structures, no uncommon words, no long phrases. The presence of God is not an abstract concept; it is rather a practical matter that is expressed in faith, love, and service. Life with God does not need intricate treatises and complex theological and philosophical concepts; it needs us to become like little children (see Matthew 18:3). This simplicity and ease remains palpable and persistent from the beginning to the end of the book even at the risk of repetitions sometimes. So there is nothing glamorous in it, but somehow it touches your heart and you feel an instant bond with its author and with God.

About Brother Lawrence

Brother Lawrence was born Nicholas Herman in French Lorraine in 1611. After he served briefly in the army and then as the footman of Monsieur de Fieubet, a government official—a task that he did not like and made him with his own admission "a clumsy oaf who broke everything" (*Presence*, 89)—he increasingly was becoming dissatisfied with what life had had to offer him. He entered the Carmelite Order at the monastery of Rue Vaugirard in Paris, which became at present part of L'Institut Catholique de Paris. This is the Order that gave to the Church and the world giants such as St. John of the Cross,

> "Brother Lawrence is well established in the affection of spiritual souls of all denominations and every shade of Christian thought."
>
> —A. W. Tozer

St. Teresa of Avila, St. Thérèse of Child Jesus—all three are doctors of the Church—and many others.

Brother Lawrence was assigned to the monastery kitchen where, amid the tedious work of cooking and cleaning, he developed his own understanding of spirituality and work: He said "that the periods of mental prayer were not at all different for him than other times" (*Presence*, 93). While working in the kitchen, he must have had in mind St. Teresa of Avila's statement, "The Lord walks among the pots and pans." God could be found in the kitchen, behind the typing machine and electronic devices, in a garage repair shop, under a tree, or behind an office desk. By presenting the universal appeal of the presence of God as a practice that crosses the lines of all human conditions, circumstances, places, and times, Brother Lawrence made an important contribution to the understanding of true spirituality.

> Brother Lawrence learned to practice the presence of God at all times and in any locations and circumstances no matter what. This is why he found inner peace and rest.

Brother Lawrence knew much pain and suffering during his eighty years of life. He was badly injured in a war fought on his native soil and was unable to return to fighting in spite of the medical care he received along with the necessary time for healing he was allowed to have. He seemed to have had one of his legs permanently crippled, and he continuously suffered pain and complications. He never complained even though his job in the kitchen required him to be on his feet, standing and moving around for hours.

Moreover, being a lay Carmelite, Brother Lawrence found himself at the lowest rung of the ladder of a system that used to favor the different levels of society; those in the lowest positions lived in the shadows and were not always treated kindly and respectfully by everyone. He learned to practice the presence of God at all times and in any locations and circumstances no matter what. This is how he found inner peace and rest. He said: "When I accepted the fact that I might spend my life suffering from these troubles and anxieties—which in no way diminished the trust I had in God and served only to increase my faith—I found myself changed all at once. And my soul, until that time always in turmoil, experienced a deep inner peace as if it had found its center and place of rest" (*Presence*, 53).

Such a conviction is perhaps rooted in the spiritual event that occurred in his early life at the age of eighteen. During one cold midwinter day, while he was looking at a leafless tree, he thought that this tree would soon be covered with leaves and it would have flowers and fruits. This simple realization filled him with "a profound insight into God's providence that has never been erased from his soul" (*Presence*, 89).

Brother Lawrence was of humble origin, and he stayed humble and simple all his life. Indeed, his outwardly life was incontestably unremarkable. He did not seem to have had an advanced formal education. He did not hear voices, perform miracles, found a new community, build a system of thought, or have prestige, high position, power, or wealth. He was not interested in titles, labels, and worldly things. So what was it about such an unglamorous individual, that attracted the special attention of the Abbé Joseph de Beaufort—Vicar of the bishop of Châlons, then Vicar General of the archbishop of Paris—who recorded the conversations he had with him, as well as the attention to many others? The answer is simple. Brother Lawrence simply loved God with all his soul, heart, strength, and will. His life attests that God is present in the most commonplace of circumstances of everyday life and that the union with God—the deepest desire of all—is possible and available for everyone to reach. So, no matter where we are in life, or what we are doing, we can and should be in the presence of God at all times. The issue is not the nature of the task we are to perform but the motivation behind it. He wrote:

> We must never tire of doing little things for the love of God who considers not the magnitude of the work, but the love. In the beginning we must not be surprised if we often fail; in the end, once the habit is formed, we will able to act without thinking about it and with great delight. (*Presence*, 98)

Were it not for this deep impression the Abbé de Beaufort felt, Brother Lawrence's life would have been in total oblivion and he would have been one of the numerous unknown saints of everyday life.

After his death, and over the years, many people added his name to the lists of the mystics, the saints, the philosophers, the innovators, and the theologians and spiritual masters. But some others labeled him as simple-minded, ignorant, uneducated, or just not even worthy of being talked about and whose book was unrealistic and redundant. In any case, his only book was short and astonishingly simple but far from being simplistic. If it was so, why is it still around more than three hundred years later? It is still there for a reason.

Furthermore, it is good that Brother Lawrence's book is called *The Practice of the Presence of God* and that the word "practice" is constantly repeated throughout the entire book. This would signal the fallibility and the struggle of our human nature. We can fail many times, but God's grace is there to help us stand up again and again. Brother Lawrence was not a marble saint and neither are we. He did not come to the full spiritual clarity and wisdom all at once. Fullness of life requires time, discipline, and continuous effort. In minutes, we can absorb intellectually the concept of the presence of God, but its practice requires a lot of constant discipline and perseverance until it "becomes more natural" (*Presence*, 76).

Suggestions for Reading This Book and Praying

The book you are holding in your hands intends to be a guide for a spiritual journey. It can be used in a retreat center, at home, or at work when you are able to secure a few moments of quiet solitude and silence. It is structured around seven days—the number of days normally used for a spiritual retreat. However, the "seven days" can be reduced to a weekend if this is all the time you can afford. It can also be spread to a much longer time if your circumstances do not allow you to have this number of hours at the same time. Anyway, the practice of the presence of God is a continuous conversation with God and an ongoing process. All that you need is your total self. God is totally present to you, and you should be totally present to God also.

Since this spiritual journey is a lifelong process, this book can be used over and over again for an even deeper immersion in the practice of the presence of God in daily life.

Each of the seven days begins with an "invitation to presence," a determination of the "focus" of the day, and a brief "opening prayer" that asks God to inspire and assist you on that particular day.

Then, there follow brief particular texts from the Scripture and passages from the writings of Brother Lawrence. Please read them slowly. Stop as soon as something—a word, a phrase, or an idea—strikes a chord in your soul. Meditate about it. Be totally with what you just read. Receive the message. Allow it to penetrate your heart and ponder it deeply. Treasure it.

The "reflection" section does not have an informative role only, but, hopefully, here you can also find inspiration that allows you to take, and persevere in, the necessary steps toward reaching the transformation and new life you are looking for. This section deals with the essence of a relationship, not just knowledge; trust, not just information; being, not just performing; growing, not just taking comfort in the zone of rites and routines; the miraculous, not just the expected; the sacredness of the ordinary, not just the mystery of the unknowable.

Now, a "pause" seems appropriate; a quotation from someone who has been there will appear as a benchmark for the steps one has taken so far and an oasis in the long, and sometimes arid and lonely, journey.

Then comes the "personal considerations" section. Please take the time you need to think about them seriously—your participation is capital. By answering the questions, you try to apply to your own daily life what you read, observed, thought about, and learned. Use the provided space for writing down your answers. By "affirmation"—if you wish, write yourself one that fits your own situation in life—you acknowledge how the presence of God is affecting you during this particular day and the days ahead.

Finally, comes the "closing prayer" that draws on some of the themes of the "day." This prayer can be used to simply end the "day" or—better—it can be used as a principal part of being in the presence of God. In this case, please read it as slowly as possible. Repeat some of its words over and over. Mean what you pray. Visualize God with you in this prayer, at that moment, at that place, and ever after and everywhere else in your daily life. You pray truly, not just with words, but with your entire life.

The format chosen here should not be restrictive by any means. It is meant to give some rhythm and regularity that can be helpful for prayer and deep reflection. You can always add to it or subtract from it according to the needs of your own personality.

This book offers you the keys of the healing power of the presence of God in the here and now. And because the self that begins a genuine spiritual journey is not the self that continues and ends the journey, you will see that at the end of the seventh day of your retreat, you will no longer find yourself in the same place as that of the first day. In the presence of God, miracles happen. Experiencing deep joy and fullness of life is one of them.

"Come and see" (see John 1:35–40) was the invitation issued by Jesus to the disciples of John who wanted to know where he dwelt. Come and sit down with Jesus and immerse yourself in the presence of God where he totally dwells. Then you will learn the art of "seeing" and living life to the fullest.

Day One

"I Will Give You Rest"

Where do you find the solution for your loneliness, worries, and unrest?

Invitation to presence: Our loving God is always in our midst. At the beginning of this spiritual journey, let us feel God's presence in a special way.

Focus: Searching for the root causes of our loneliness, worries, and restlessness.

Opening Prayer: Reverently, I enter into this sacred time of prayer and reflection. Make me aware, dear God, of your divine presence in my life. I come to you with all my concerns and burdens, but I come. Help me to enter into true rest—your rest.

Scripture Reading

Come to me, all you that are weary and are carrying heavy burdens, and I will give you rest. Take my yoke upon you, and learn from me; for I am gentle and humble in heart, and you will find rest for your souls. For my yoke is easy, and my burden is light. (Matthew 11:28–30)

Cast your burden on the Lord, and he will sustain you. (Psalm 55:22)

What do mortals get from all the toil and strain with which they toil under the sun? For all their days are full of pain, and their work is a vexation; even at night their minds do not rest. This also is vanity. (Ecclesiastes 2:22–23)

Learning from Brother Lawrence

How happy we would be if we could only find the treasure of which the gospel speaks; nothing else would matter. Since it is inexhaustible, the more we search, the more riches we find. Let us devote ourselves ceaselessly to looking for it; let us not grow weary until we have found it. . . . (*Presence*, 61)

I know that to do this [practicing the presence of God] your heart must be empty of all other things because God desires to possess it exclusively, and he cannot possess it exclusively without first emptying it of everything other than himself; neither can he act within it nor do there what he pleases. (*Presence*, 57)

I cannot understand how religious people can remain content without the practice of the presence of God. As for me, I keep myself recollected in him in the depth and center of my soul as much as possible, and when I am thus with him I fear nothing, though the least deviation is hell for me. (*Presence*, 59)

Reflection

You certainly know the feeling—who doesn't? It is that feeling of emptiness, loneliness, and brokenness of heart—and it hurts.

We often feel as if no one understands us, no one loves us, and no one cares for us. We feel that generosity seems always one-sided; we do everything for others and not one reciprocates anything, and if we were sensitive enough, we would grasp the depth of the isolation and disconnection and measure the height and length of the walls around us.

If you never felt this way, lucky you, you are something else. If you felt it, welcome to the human race. For all ages, all nations, all classes, and for both men and women, loneliness has been a problem. We feel ready to do anything to fill the void. The feeling of emptiness is not only painful; it is scary.

Needless to say how some circumstances of our lives make things even worse. These circumstances are numerous and of many kinds that include, for example, death; divorce; loss of a position or a job; being a member of a certain religious, ethical, or minority group; having a physical or mental handicap; or feeling a social outcast for a reason or no reason at all.

Moreover, our feeling of loneliness becomes even sharper in an individualistic society and highly competitive society such as ours which makes us experience a deep, sometimes desperate, need to belong—to something much larger than our ego.

So what to do with that terrible hole in our soul and heart?

Some of us choose to be bitter about it and seek other individuals who happen to be in the same situation to just lament and complain and become depressed. Some prefer to withdraw and fill their minds with fantasies and unrealistic dreams. Some join gangs, addict to alcohol and drugs and "thrills," use sexual partners, or just marry even for the wrong reasons. Most of us, however, fill the void with continuous "noises," all kind of activities, legitimate achievements, and even commendable religious practices and rituals.

But all these tools are "temporary fixes." They do not reach the root causes of the problem, nor do they last. This is why we keep wanting more and more and always more.

I want to know, as much as you do I'm sure, that I am not alone in my life. Amid the hectic pace of everyday life, the pressure of the ever-demanding workplace, of raising a family, and of social obligations, and under the burdens of all kinds of worries and aggravations that are too heavy to be borne alone, I want to be sure I am not alone. I do have an anxious fear of aloneness and of this "emptiness" feeling, and I want to "fill" it with something as quickly as possible. A fullness of life—the sign of God's presence—is the only way that remedies the bottomless sense of absence we are subjected to. Then unexpected things happen. Roger Schutz, the prior of the Taizé community once wrote:

> . . . you are never alone. Let yourself be plumbed to the depths, and you will realize that everyone is created for a presence. There in your heart of hearts, in that place where not two people are alike, Christ is waiting for you. And there the unexpected happens.

Basically, we are crying out for the Infinite without realizing that the Infinite cannot be substituted with just the accumulation of the finites. We seem constantly driven by the

> Basically, we are crying out for the Infinite without realizing that the Infinite cannot be substituted with just the accumulation of the finites.

latest, the newest, the greatest, the most exhilarating, and the number one in anything. But never any of these was able to satisfy anyone. Never. That is why we keep wanting more and more, as if there is an end to the "more and more" myth, until the moment we find the Infinite. The Infinite was always there, but we did not know it or we did not admit to it.

Brother Lawrence was so dissatisfied with the ways of the world and all that life had to offer that he withdrew in a Carmelite monastery hoping to find something else. He found the peace and rest he was looking for in the simple and hidden life of service in the kitchen. He found God and he practiced the presence of God for the rest of his life.

In the presence of God, Brother Lawrence felt neither lonely, nor brokenhearted, nor bored. In the presence of God, he did not find a difference between his time in prayer and his time in the kitchen. Everything became a continual conversation with God. He did not need to fill an empty spot because, having God in his heart and mind, he did not feel the void. God was all he needed.

> In the presence of God, Brother Lawrence felt neither lonely, nor brokenhearted, nor bored.

God is all we need too.

The bottom line is this: a distracted life has no center and when we turn away from something, we turn toward something else. When we turn away from the fundamental questions of our existence for fear of having to confront them, we turn toward activities, habits, attitudes, and achievements as a solution for our problems. It is not easy to deal with questions such as "Who am I? Why am I here? Where am I going?" So we leave them on the back burner, and we convince ourselves and others that we are busy doing things and we do not have time left to do other things that happen to be the essential things. We hide in the thick bushes of our psychologically and socially constructed false self, and we do not want to hear God's voice when he is wandering in our inner garden, proposing his companionship to us, "Where are you?" (Genesis 3:9).

We are ever burdened with physical, intellectual, emotional, and sometimes even spiritual "staffs." We are immersed in an ocean of worries, sadness, ambition, shame, guilt, isolation, alienation, and exasperations. We are reduced to simple commodities; things—and even people— are appreciated in proportion of their "usefulness" because our culture tends to dispose of the "useless." We are exhausted and depleted.

> There is a hidden contemplative spirit in each one of us even though we often are not aware of its existence.

The rest and refreshment we long for cannot be of this world. The things of this world just mask dissatisfaction and pains. Deep down in each soul there is a longing—a kind of archetypal energy—for the infinite. There is a hidden contemplative spirit in each one of us even though we often are not aware of its existence.

After describing his many years of guilt, despair, and depression, Brother Lawrence turned to God with Jesus' invitation certainly in mind, "Come to me, all you that are weary and are carrying heavy burdens, and I will give you rest" (Matthew 11:24). Then he wrote:

> When I accepted the fact that I might spend my life suffering from these troubles and anxieties—which in no way diminished the trust I had in God and served only to increase my

faith—I found myself changed all at once. And my soul, until that time always in turmoil, experienced a deep inner peace as if it had found its center and place of rest. (*Presence*, 53)

Loneliness, emptiness, and brokenness of heart can be frightening. Indeed, they are. But they can be looked at as gifts from God too. They can be opportunities for insight and growth. They can be seen as a call deep within our being telling us what we should do and what we should not do. But we have to listen. To listen efficiently requires a certain degree of silence—both within and without. We live in a noisy world. We fill our world with noise maybe because we are afraid to face ourselves. In his book, *Beginning to Pray*, Orthodox Archbishop Anthony Bloom wrote these insightful lines about the threat of silence:

> Try to find time to stay alone with yourself: shut the door and settle down in your room at a moment when you have nothing else to do. Say "I am now with myself," and just sit with yourself. After an amazingly short time you will most likely feel bored. This teaches us one very useful thing. It gives us insight into the fact that if after ten minutes of being alone with ourselves we feel like that, it is no wonder that others should feel equally bored! Why is this so? It is so because we have so little to offer to our own selves as food for thought, for emotion and for life. If you watch your life carefully you will discover quite soon that we hardly ever live from within outwards; instead we respond to incitement, to excitement. In other words, we live by reflection, by reaction. Something happens and we respond, someone speaks and we answer. But when we are left without anything that stimulates us to

think, speak or act, we realise that there is very little in us that will prompt us to action in any direction at all. This is really a very dramatic discovery. We are completely empty, we do not act from within ourselves but accept as our life a life which is actually fed in from outside; we are used to things happening which compel us to do other things. How seldom can we live simply by means of the depth and the richness we assume that there is within ourselves. (Mahwah, NJ: Paulist Press, 1970, pp. 67–68)

The truth is that by learning to listen we can become attentive to God's presence and action in us and through and around us. We become aware of his presence in all of life. Then, as Henri Nouwen put it so well,

Wherever I am, at home, in a hotel, in a train, plane or airport, I would not feel irritated, restless, and desirous of being somewhere else or doing something else. I would know that here and now is what counts and is important because it is God himself who wants me at this time and in this place.

We become assured of God's company—by all accounts the best and most relaxing company there is. Christ said it clearly, "And remember, I am with you always, to the end of the age" (Matthew 28:20).

Pause: Ponder Jean Vanier's thought: "Even the most beautiful community can never heal the wound of loneliness that we carry. It is only when we discover that this loneliness can become a sacrament that we touch wisdom, for this sacrament is purification and presence of God."

Personal Considerations

1. Find a quiet place. Gently close your eyes. Be still. Take a deep breath. Clear your mind. Now, do you feel alone with the Alone or is your inner world flooded with ideas, memories, images, fantasies, plans, realized and unrealized dreams, and especially unforgettable hurts that make you vulnerable and lonely and tired of it all? Then, think about where to go from here. Set your goals for releasing the yoke of loneliness, toil, and unrest this week.

---

2. Do you think primarily about yourself, others, or God when you make decisions? Whom, in the heart of your heart, do you try to please? Make a little inventory of your qualities, habits, and attitudes by listing who you are today. Then review this list and revise it under who you are when you rest in God's presence. Then check off all the qualities on both lists that reflect your true self. Meditate upon these qualities for seven days to integrate them more fully.

---

3. Many of us seem to be threatened by silence and solitude. We seek protection from them by surrounding ourselves with noise—radio, television, stereo, chatter or any other type of distraction—or with busyness—work or pretense-work. In order to know ourselves more deeply, we need time for reflection in silence and solitude. To assess the quality of your life, list the busyness or your life on the left and the silence and solitude of your life on the right.

_____

_____

_____

_____

4. After you assess the above lists, what steps can you take to nurture your life with more silence and solitude and deep reflection?

_____

_____

_____

_____

Affirmation: *God is the source of my serenity, health, and vitality. I am at peace.*

Now, create a relevant affirmation of your own based on your experience and/or the above personal considerations.

Closing Prayer

O God, my God,

Take all you have given me; I am yours.

Take my liberty, my memory, my understanding, and my
entire will.

Take also my pretenses, my opinions, my conclusions,
my disappointments, my frustration, and my bitter
loneliness.

Show me the traps I tend to fall into and the difference
between facts and myths.

Inspire me to replace my negative reactions with the
reality of your plan for me.

Be with me when I stand alone in the path of seeking
to do what is right. How often I stand alone, my
dear Lord, with no one to understand me! But you do.
I feel fully and intimately known by you. How can I
be alone?

Be with me when my family and my friends and my
so-called friends turn their back and seem oblivious to
my needs and when they are not there to support me
and encourage me. But I know you are always there
for me, and I can always count on you to answer my
prayer. Yes I know.

Give me this great assurance of your grace so that I
can reject my unhealthy patterns from the past, my
disillusioned interpretations from the present, and
my unrealistic dreams for the future.

Day by day and hour by hour, help me to live in your divine presence. You are "my strength and my shield; in him my heart trusts; so I am helped, and my heart exults, and with my song I give thanks to him" (Psalm 28:7).

Make me wise enough to put no limitations on your infinite power for continuing to create me and shape me and transform me. Build when I build, write when I write, walk when I walk, eat when I eat, play when I play, and always do whatever I do, so that I can do what you do.

Thank you, my Lord, for your greatest gift—the pleasure of your company. I am never alone. Amen!

Now, write your own personalized closing prayer for today based on "I Will Give You Rest."

Day Two

"There Is Need of Only One Thing"

Are you running from God instead of to God?

Invitation to presence: Let us remember that the Holy Spirit of God who empowers our lives wants to inspire and be present in our decisions here and now.

Focus: Reexamining our priorities.

Opening Prayer: Lord, you know how easily I substitute the blessing of your presence with so many activities and distractions. Help me to imitate Mary, whose greatest desire was to be in your presence.

Scripture Reading

Martha, Martha, you are worried and distracted by many things; there is need of only one thing. Mary has chosen the better part, which will not be taken away from her. (Luke 10:41–42)

There is still one thing lacking. Sell all that you own and distribute the money to the poor, and you will have treasure in heaven; then come, follow me. (Luke 18:22)

One thing I asked of the Lord, that will I seek after: to live in the house of the Lord all the days of my life, to behold the beauty of the Lord, and to inquire in his temple. (Psalm 27:4)

Learning from Brother Lawrence

> Let us commit ourselves entirely to him, and banish everything else from our hearts and minds. He wants to be alone there, so we should ask him for this grace. If we do what we can, we will soon see the change we hope for in ourselves. (*Presence*, 83–84)

> His [Brother Lawrence's] principal concern throughout the more than forty years he has been in religious life has been always to be with God, and to do, say, or think nothing that could displease him. He has no other interest than the pure love of God who deserves infinitely more besides. (*Presence*, 49)

> Let us often recall . . . that our only concern in this life is to please God, and that everything else is folly and vanity. (*Presence*, 67)

Reflection

Sooner or later, and in one way or another, most of us are faced with existential and critical questions such as: "Who am I? What am I? Why am I? What am I really looking for? What is my reason for being? What am I seeking? What are the motivations of my actions? What is the point of living?" We cannot escape the urgency of these questions for as Socrates put it, "The unexamined life is not worth living." He also was credited to have said, "Know thyself."

Such questions need attention and answers. Even though most of us do not conceptualize the answers, consciously or unconsciously we live the answers without being aware that we have been doing it.

Many of us count on false concepts of God: a mythological "God" up in the far sky, a statue of "God," a graven image of "God," a fantasy or an abstract concept of "God," or on just following certain rules of conduct to please a certain "God" of their making. Instead of believing that they are created in the image of God, these individuals seem to have created God in their own image. God becomes the fruit of their imagination and the driven force of their ideology. Their conception of God (theology) drives their conception of the human nature (anthropology), which, in turn, conditions the social order they want.

Many others—perhaps most of us—try to avoid dealing directly with the most important questions of our lives by keeping ourselves too busy reaching goals, achieving results, and doing the "right thing" out of duty or according to the requirements of the moment. Who would blame Martha, for example, for doing what a host was supposed to do for a guest, especially if the guest was Jesus? But Jesus said: "Martha, Martha, you are worried and distracted by many things; there is need of only one thing. Mary has chosen the better part, which will not be taken away from her" (Luke 10:41–42).

If we do not have this one thing needed, no matter what we do, we will be left dissatisfied and restless. The truth is that all these things we think are important to us and occupy our attention and time are results, not causes. This is why they are supposed to be secondary, not primary. So, aims, goals, and achievements do not necessarily explain life. The end—this "there is need of only one thing"—should be the starting point that explains the rest of life.

Since the beginning God commanded his people to worship no other gods (see Exodus 20:3). Jesus said we cannot serve two masters (see Matthew 6:24) nor can we love both God and wealth (see Matthew 6:24). He also wanted us to put God ahead of family (see Luke 14:26), ourselves (see Luke 14:26), and everything else (see Luke 14:33). Therefore, we have to clean house of all other gods because our heart cannot be crowded; it has room for only one god—the true God.

> Anything that stands between us and God is the new idol, and no matter what we call it, it is an idol because it takes the place of God in our life.

We do not think of ourselves as worshipers of idols. Oh! Certainly not us. We think that idolatry belongs to pagan cultures or to the ancient past. But, to our surprise perhaps it is here under different names. Anything that stands between us and God is the new idol, and no matter what we call it, it is an idol because it takes the place of God in our life.

We have private gods. We have national gods. We have global gods. They are blatant or subtle, mental or emotional, and spiritual or physical. They have specific names that include money, busyness, competition, comfort and instant gratification, appearance and consumerism, sexual freedom and choice, individualism and relativism. They also include secular humanism and materialism, success, prestige, power, overemphasis on the role of science, pick-and-choose cafeteria type of religions, and possessions such as clothes, houses, electronic devices, cars, and many more like these. You've got the idea.

Even though it can be neutral first, every time we allow any one of these to enter in competition with God, we fashion a "gold calf" (see Exodus 32) and we worship it, or we can go even further and deny God altogether by believing that we can do as the serpent suggested, "You will be like God" (Genesis 3:5). And we go reliving this first delusion again and again, led astray and taken "captive through philosophy and empty deceit, according to human tradition, according to the elemental spirits of the universe, and not according to Christ" (Colossians 2:8). So we become accustomed to running from God instead of running to him.

Another danger consists in envisioning God as a kind of a cosmic Santa Claus who meets our wants on certain occasions or when we meet certain conditions, or a kind of vending machine that gives us what we choose when we use the right token. Even though we know that such a God does not exist, we keep doing it without realizing that this provides proofs and ammunition to agnostic and Freudian followers who want to reduce the entire God concept to a father figure concept or to just a projection of unrealized wishes. Then we are confused. A confused person is "like a foolish man who built his house on sand. The rain fell, and the flood came, and the winds blew and beat against that house, and it fell—and great was the fall!" (Matthew 7:26–27) This is what happens when we lose our references and all solid ground possible. Before praying the Angelus on June 1, 2008, Pope Benedict XVI said in his greeting:

> Every person needs a "center" in his life, a source of truth and goodness to draw from in the flux of the different situations of everyday life and its toil. Everyone of us, when he pauses for a moment of silence, needs to feel not only the beating of his own heart, but more deeply, the beating of a trustworthy presence, perceptible to the senses of faith and yet more real: the presence of Christ, heart of the world.

Brother Lawrence, in the footsteps of many other men and women, tried to have room in his heart for the true God—the "only one thing" needed, the "center," and the only solid reference. For him it is not what we have and accomplish that really counts; it is all about loving God. We are made to love God. We exist to love God. Our fundamental purpose is to love God, and we will continue to be restless and dissatisfied until we truly love God.

> Brother Lawrence, in the footsteps of many other men and women, tried to have room in his heart for the true God—the "only one thing" needed, the "center," and the only solid reference.

Therefore, our number one priority is our love for God. This is the love that gives value to anything else we do in our lives. Our love for God is enough and more than enough, as sooner or later we will realize.

Moreover, it is our love for God that will allow us to really know God. The "God is love" of St. John (1 John 4:16) suggests that God wants to be known with "heart knowledge" more than with "head knowledge." God understands and is understood by the language of the heart more than by the language of the intellect.

The belief in God that is based on information and impressions from early learning and education, and then colored by cultural bias, does not necessarily mean that we know God. Although this kind of knowledge by hearsay has, of course, its own obvious value and is very common and successful in many cases, it remains, however, as evasive as any of the worldly tenets of a culture. Besides God himself, no one and nothing can reveal the true God to us. God wants his children to personally know him. When we realize that we can and must have a personal relationship with God through a loving heart, we discover that all other knowledge is in fact less relevant than we first thought. A loving heart, even without words, knows more about God and about others than any persuasive speech and sophisticated method without a loving heart. The knowledge obtained by love is the deepest, the truest, and the most relevant because it is the knowledge of a relationship with God. A relationship with God is by far more important and dynamic than any information about God. It is, in essence, about being and becoming.

> A relationship with God is by far more important and dynamic than any information about God. It is, in essence, about being and becoming.

Sometimes we become aware that we have been for a long, long time on an intensive search for the truth, and we have been using all kinds of methods, courses, theories, and complicated procedures, and we realize how much they promise and how little they deliver. Then what? Brother Lawrence solution is this:

> In several books I found different methods to approach God and various practices of the spiritual life that I feared would burden my mind rather than facilitate what I wanted and what I sought, namely, a means of being completely disposed to God. This led me to resolve to give all for all. Thus, after offering myself entirely to God in atonement for my sins, I renounced for the sake of his love everything other than God, and I began to live as if only he an I existed in the world. (*Presence*, 75)

So, the best way to go to God—and this will certainly work—is to turn our whole heart and will to him. Intellect can certainly be important, but by itself and because of its limits, it only gets us so far. The deepest truths are proved through the heart and by living in the presence of God. The intellect alone cannot grasp all such a living is made of. It is in the heart where we meet God. And it is this kind of deep knowing and true love that helps us to "keep [ourselves] from idols" (1 John 5:21). When we discover who God truly is, we will discover who we truly are.

Pause. Ponder St. Augustine's memorable sentence, "[O Lord,] You have made us for yourself, and our hearts are restless until they can find peace in you."

Personal Considerations

1. In your everyday life, are you running from God or to God? On the left, list ways you are running from God; on the right, list ways you are running to God.

   _____

   _____

   _____

   _____

2. What is keeping you from living in the presence of God in your everyday life? What steps can you take today to improve the situation?

   _____

   _____

   _____

   _____

3. Do you feel ready to "sell" all that you have and "buy" the field where the "treasure" is hidden according to the Gospel (see Matthew 13:44) because as Brother Lawrence said, "Our heart will be where our treasure is" (*Presence*, 68)? What "attachments" or "idols" do you need to release in order to put God first in your life?

_____

_____

_____

_____

Affirmation: *No matter what I do, my main concern remains to be in God's presence.*

Now, create a relevant affirmation of your own based on your experience and/or the above personal considerations.

Closing Prayer

Thank you, Lord, for revealing to me the danger of busyness, accumulation of "successes," and the multiple distractions that invade my life. Deliver me from pursuing the flawed agenda of status, power, position, or recognition.

Grant that I may discern at all times, even when things are going very well, but especially in the darkest moments, grant, Lord, that I discern and recognize the signs of your presence.

Grant me the gift of focusing in you so that I can understand that it is you, not myself and especially not my abilities and activities, who really count.

Help me to overcome the tendency of letting other people set my values, my goals, and my schedule.

Teach me to sit at your feet and learn the secret of the "only one thing" that is needed and that comes only from you. I don't want to know how, when, why, and where; all that I want to know is who, and that's you. Be real to me. Then I know that with you I am protected, supported, and well guided.

My dear Lord, I know that you know better than I do and that you have the answer. "Lord, Lord to where can [I] go?" (John 6:68). You are "the way, and the truth, and the life" (John 14:6). You are the answer.

Let your love be the power that gives life to my life. Amen!

Now, write your own personalized closing prayer for today based on "There Is Need for Only One Thing."

Day Three

The "Aha!" Moment: Getting a Life Now

Have you had any big wake-up calls in life?

Invitation to presence: The God who is the Lord of all things and who knows and understands everything about us and about all other things is with us where we are in life here and now.

Focus: Living fully.

Opening Prayer: Lord, earthly treasures left me feeling dissatisfied and emptier than ever. Please fill my immense longing with your infinite presence so I can live fully.

Scripture Reading

I am the way, and the truth, and the life. (John 14:6)

I came that they may have life, and have it abundantly. (John 10:10)

It is no longer I who live, but it is Christ who lives in me. And the life I now live in the flesh I live by faith in the Son of God, who loved me and gave himself for me. (Galatians 2:20)

Learning from Brother Lawrence

I keep myself recollected in him in the depth and center of my soul as much as possible, and when I am thus with him I fear nothing, though the least deviation is hell for me. (*Presence*, 59)

How happy we would be if we could find the treasure of which the gospel speaks; nothing else would matter. Since it is inexhaustible, the more we search, the more riches we find. Let us devote ourselves ceaselessly to looking for it; let us not grow weary until we have found it. . . . (*Presence*, 61)

> "Presenting myself like a stone before the divine Sculptor, I beg Him to form His perfect image in my soul and make me entirely like Him."
>
> —*Presence*, 95

Regarding the prescribed hours of prayer, they are nothing more than a continuation of this same exercise. Sometimes I think of myself as a piece of stone before a sculptor who desires to carve a statue; presenting myself in this way before God I ask him to fashion his perfect image in my soul, making me entirely like himself. (*Presence*, 54)

Reflection

King David, like any other king, queen, president, or any other influential leader, became ultimately disillusioned by a life of power, pleasure, wealth, and prestige. Something deep and abiding was missing from his life; his heart seemed devoid of the deep joy he hoped to find in his worldly achievements and material success. Finally, he turned his face to God.

King David summarized the situation by saying to the Lord: "In your presence there is fullness of joy; in your right hand are pleasures forevermore" (Psalm 16:11). He had discovered the mystery of the fullness of life: the only all-satisfying happiness cannot be found outside a genuine intimacy with God.

Brother Lawrence spent more than forty years as a Brother whose concern was "always to be with God, and to do, say, or think nothing that could displease him" (*Presence*, 49). He then can attest:

> There is no way of life in the world more agreeable or delightful than continual conversation with God; only those who practice and experience it can understand this. I do not suggest, however, that you do it for this reason. We must not seek consolations from this exercise, but must do it from a motive of love, and because God wants it. (*Presence*, 57)

Somehow, practicing the presence of God gives a sense of relief and a great joy because one realizes that:

- God is in charge;
- God is our Father and we can talk to him directly, personally, continually, and in a simple way;
- God could be met right here right now, in this place and moment, and not in some far sky, or past memory, or distant future, because the present moment is the presence of God and the meeting point with his will;
- God can use anyone of us, even the weakest among us;
- God never abandons us, even if we abandon him—Jesus promised: "I am with you always, to the end of the age" (Mathew 28:20);

- God is the source of every gift we have, and he will give us more if we ask him for more;
- God does not only give us life, but his is our life, and this is all we need; and
- When we have a close relationship with God, everything else within us and around us seems to fall in place and we have harmony and peace even in chaotic and confusing situations.

Brother Lawrence wrote: "During the first ten years I suffered a great deal. . . . During this period I fell often, but I got back up just as quickly. It seemed to me that all creatures, reason, and God himself were against me, and that faith alone was on my side" (*Presence*, 52–53). But then, something else happened—his "aha!" moment of freedom and continual joy. Filled with the indwelling presence of God, he spent the next thirty years of his life, during sickness and health, and amid aggravations and daily work in the kitchen with all its duties—a work he did not particularly appreciate, but he did it anyway for the love of God—in great peace, tranquility, and delight. He lived the present moment where he met God's will and engaged in a continual conversation with God. This is how he saw it:

> I gave up all devotions and prayers that were not required and I devote myself exclusively to remaining always in his holy presence. I keep myself in his presence by simple attentiveness and a general loving awareness of God that I call "actual presence of God" or better, a quiet and secret conversation of the soul with God that is lasting. This sometimes results in interior, and often exterior, contentment and joys so great that I have to perform childish acts, appearing more

like folly than devotion, to control them and keep them from showing outwardly. (*Presence*, 53)

It is worth noticing here that this type of continual conversation with God comes often under different names in the history of spirituality. These names include, for example, prayer without ceasing, prayer of the heart, mental prayer, contemplative prayer, meditative prayer, centering prayer, interior prayer . . . which all practice the presence of God even though from more or less different angles. Brother Lawrence himself tried to give different names for his experience. He said:

I know someone (Brother Lawrence is referring to himself here) who, for forty years, has practiced an intellectual presence of God to which he gives several other names. Sometimes he calls it a "simple act," a "clear and distinct knowledge of God," an "indistinct view" or a general and loving awareness of God." Other times he names it "attention to God," "silent conversation with God," "trust in God," or "the soul's life and peace." This person told me that all these forms of God's presence are nothing but synonyms for the same thing, and that it is at present second nature to him. (*Presence*, 39–40)

Brother Lawrence must have had in mind the words of Christ, "Peace I leave with you; my peace I give you. I do not give to you as the world gives. . . . So that in me you may have peace" (John 14:27; 16:33) when he wrote: "My soul, until that time always in turmoil, experienced a deep inner peace as if it had found its center and place of rest" (*Presence*, 53).

When we have this kind of sweet peace that is the result of God's grace, without which nothing exists, and the practice of his presence in us, we no longer have room for evil intruders such as bitterness, resentment, envy, jealousy, hostility, arrogance, and the feeling of emptiness, meaningless, and absurdity. Instead, it is Christ's joy that will remain in us, and it will be complete (see John 15:11).

Upon visiting her cousin Elizabeth, Mary praised God saying:

> My soul magnifies the Lord, and my spirit rejoices in God my Savior, for he has looked with favor on the lowliness of his servant. Surely, from now on all generations will call me blessed; for the Mighty One has done great things for me, and holy is his name. His mercy is for those who fear him from generation to generation. He has shown strength with his arm; he has scattered the proud in the thoughts of their hearts. He has brought down the powerful from their thrones, and lifted up the lowly; he has filled the hungry with good things, and sent the rich away empty. He has helped his servant Israel, in remembrance of his mercy, according to the promise he made to our ancestors, to Abraham and to his descendants forever. (Luke 1:46–55)

At reading these words, one cannot but conclude that Mary loved God with all her heart, soul, mind, and strength as perfectly as a human being is capable of. And God selected her to be the mother of his Son. She was the favored one. The angel assured her, "Greetings, favored one! The Lord is with you . . . Do not be afraid, Mary, for your have found favor with God" (Luke 1:28–30). There is no greater delight than rejoicing in God (see Luke 1:47), for God is most pleased with those who please him (see Luke 1:28).

Our "Yes" to God, like Brother Lawrence's and Mary's "Yes," can be our the source of our true happiness. Our "Yes" brings the poverty of our lives into the richness of God's generosity and plans for us. It brings us to conform our lives to Jesus' life. Foolishly, we thought that our happiness came from living life our way. Wrong. True happiness comes only from living life God's way. Therefore, our fulfillment lies in the abolishment of our agendas of fulfillment and in the conformity to the values of Christ's kingdom, which turn the values of the world upside down.

> True happiness comes only from living life God's way.

When we delight in God alone, our minds and hearts are so changed that our needs and wants change also. Our thoughts and desires become the same as Jesus'.

There is an old adage that says, "As within, so without." It means that what we experience in our outer world—opportunities, relationships, careers, and perhaps circumstances themselves—can be the reflection of what is happening inside ourselves. Also, what is happening outside tends to influence greatly our moods and way of thinking. So if we are interiorly anchored on the reality that does not change—the Creator and God of love—we will build our life from this vision of the Creator and God of love a vision that can be more real than the reality we know through our senses. The vision of the unseen Truth and Beauty is what makes us truly alive and full of joy. We belong to two worlds: the within and the without. Regardless of how "perfect" our life may appear to be, filled with good events and luck, and how genuine and

> When we delight in God alone, our minds and hearts are so changed that our needs and wants change also.

wonderful people we deal with are, this outer world is never enough. Nothing in the outer world can satisfy the longings and desires of the soul. Our challenge is to radiate exteriorly what we are interiorly, that we are true children of God. This would be the deepest joy and the fullness of life we are ever able to experience. By practicing the presence of God daily, we can live every day in the "peak" of God's fullness.

Pause: Consider the recommendation of St. Francis of Assisi, "Let the brothers ever avoid appearing gloomy, sad, and clouded, like the hypocrites; but let one ever be found joyous in the Lord, gay, amiable, gracious, as is meet."

Personal Considerations

1. Do you feel the presence of God in your life today? Do you feel you are present to God today? What "Aha!" moments have led you to change your way of living your life? What steps did you take in order to live your new life?

   _____

   _____

   _____

   _____

2. Have you had peak experiences in your life of great inner joy, love, and peace? What precipitated these experiences? Explain.

   _____

   _____

   _____

   _____

3. What would your life look like if you lived your life the
   way St. Paul put it, "It is no longer I who live, but it is
   Christ who lives in me" (Galatians 2:20)?

   _____

   _____

   _____

   _____

Affirmation: *I am experiencing God's life in my life.*

Now, create a relevant affirmation of your own based on
your experience and/or the above personal considerations.

Closing Prayer

Father in heaven and everywhere, I acknowledge your
presence in all things, and all I want from you at this
moment is the realization of your divine presence—
not for any other reason, just for the joy of being in
your presence.

Being closer to me than my own breath—"[You are]
closer to us than we think" wrote you servant Brother
Lawrence—and even before I lift my eyes or thoughts
to you or utter a single word, you know all my needs,
my all-knowing and all-compassionate Lord.

So, I turn to you now, not to reveal to you the list of
my needs—all my needs are palpable to you—but to
receive the fulfillment of my essential need; I can no
longer live without your holy and fulfilling presence.

I come to you now, not seeking more things, not seeking
different circumstances, not seeking even change and

improvement, but seeking the only fulfilling desire there is—the gift of yourself.

When I live in your presence, I won't have life on my own to live; you will live my life. Then I will live the fullness of life. Then my joy will be complete.

Thank you for allowing me to perceive the beauty of your manifestation everywhere I look and for teaching me how to look at things.

Thank you for allowing me to savor the fullness of life. Now I understand the explosion of joy uttered by the psalmist, "This is the day that the Lord has made; let us rejoice and be glad in it" (Psalm 118:24).

In your presence, Father, teach me to always keep a grateful heart and to get out of your way. Amen!

Now, write your own personalized closing prayer for today based on living a life in God as expressed in "The 'Aha!' Moment: Getting a Life Now."

Day Four

God's Policy and Our Response: Total Involvement

Do you have a reciprocal relationship with God?

Invitation to presence: The all-powerful God of the universe dwells within us in whatever we are and do.

Focus: To keep God as the center of our being is to keep God in mind and heart at all times.

Opening Prayer: O God, make me learn to attend to your presence, like Jesus, in all that I think and do. I thank you for your ongoing creation of me, and I ask you to grant me the grace of doing things in union with you moment by moment.

Scripture Reading

Apart from me you can do nothing. (John 15:5)

Truly I tell you, just as you did it to one of the least of these who are members of my family, you did it to me. (Matthew 25:40)

You shall love the Lord your God with all your heart, and with all your soul, and with all your mind, and with all your strength. (Mark 12:30; see also Deuteronomy 6:5)

Learning from Brother Lawrence

A soul depends on grace in proportion to its desire for greater perfection. God's help is necessary at every moment because without it the soul can do nothing. The world, nature, and the devil together wage war so fiercely and so relentlessly that, without this special help and this humble, necessary dependence, they would carry off the soul against its will. This seems contrary to nature, but grace finds pleasure and peace therein. (*Presence*, 36)

[Brother Lawrence said] that he had always been governed by love with no other interest, never worrying whether he would be damned or saved, and having once decided to perform all his actions for the love of God, he was at peace. He was content even when picking up a straw from the ground for the love of God, seeking him alone and nothing else, not even his gifts. (*Presence*, 91)

> "Having once decided to perform all his actions for the love of God, he [Brother Lawrence] was at peace. He was content even when picking up a straw from the ground for the love of God, seeking him alone and nothing else, not even his gifts."
>
> —*Presence*, 91

The same was true of the kitchen to which he [Brother Lawrence] had the strongest natural aversion. He got used to doing everything for the love of God, asking him at every opportunity for the grace to do his work. He was able to carry it out with great ease for the fifteen years he was in charge of it.

He was assigned to the sandal shop, which was a delight for him, but he was willing to give up this task like the others. He would find joy everywhere doing little things for the love of God. (*Presence*, 93)

Reflection

God wants to be totally involved in our lives as much as he wants us to be totally involved in his life. There is no rest except in God, as St. Augustine said. We limit God's action when we do not open up to this reality.

When we allow God to do with us whatever he wants to do, we become receptive to his grace at all levels of our existence. His grace then will be at work not only for our salvation but also in the long journey of our transformation and sanctification.

"Unless the Lord builds the house," the psalmist reminds us, "those who build it labor in vain. Unless the Lord builds the city, the guard keeps watch in vain" (Psalm 127:1). What the psalm is saying is that God wants to be involved in whatever we are doing. If we've got a house to build, God wants to build it. If we've got a business to run, God wants to run it. If we've got a country to govern, God wants to be the leader of the country. If we've got a family to take care of, God wants to be the Lord of the home. There is nothing unimportant to him. He is concerned about every detail of our life—God is the Lord of the details—and wants to be involved in every aspect of it. He wants us to do everything his way for he is the way (see John 14:6). His way leads to lasting fulfillment and eternal happiness. Our ways do not. The disciples could not find fish until Jesus told them, "Cast the net to the right side of the boat, and you will find some" (John 21:6).

When we bring God into the so-called mundane, the mundane will no longer be mundane; it becomes sacred. This is why St. Paul can write: "Whether you eat or drink, or whatever you do, do everything for the glory of God" (1 Corinthians 10:31). This is why for Brother Lawrence, "It is a big mistake to think that the period of mental prayer should be different from any other" (*Presence*, 98), and, therefore, life is not to be divided into activity of prayer and activity of balancing our checkbook as if these two activities are meant to exclude each other. They do not. God wants to be present in every area of our life whether we are meditating or just flipping burgers. What we do is not really the most important thing. What gives real value to our action is how, for whom, and to what purpose we do what we do. This is why we can transform all our activities into prayer.

> God wants to be present in every area of our life whether we are meditating or just flipping burgers.

Therefore, as we approach our own responsibilities—no matter what they are—we are to surrender them to God, who is in charge and in control of everything, and bend our will to his will. In any circumstance of our lives, we should be able to say: "God, you are in total control of my family, home, business, plans, future. I give them all to you. Build them the way you wish them to be built." Then we are praying without ceasing (see 1 Thessalonians 5:17) and having an unbroken conversation with God.

> What we do is not really the most important thing. What gives real value to our action is how, for whom, and to what purpose we do what we do. This is why we can transform all our activities into prayer.

Total surrender to God's will is, in fact, the best cure for self-deception we, at different degrees, are familiar with. When we place ourselves in God's hands, we can be certain that whatever happens is in God's plan for us and that our Father knows what is best for his children even though it can be beyond our immediate understanding. François Fénelon wrote:

> Let God act. Abandon yourself to Him. You will suffer, but you will suffer with love, peace and consolation. You will fight, but you can carry off the victory, and God Himself will crown you with His own hand. You will weep, but your tears will be sweet, and God Himself will come to dry them.
>
> You will not be free any longer to give yourself up to your tyrannic passions, but you will sacrifice your liberty freely, and you will enter into a new liberty unknown to the world in which you will do nothing except for love of God.

If we entrust the driving force in our lives to God, we will be safe because he has the right map that leads to our destination. And if problems arise along the way, he will figure out the solution, for he is the answer. No worrying from our part is necessary. We should always remember what the Scripture recommends, "Trust in the Lord with all your heart and do not rely on your insight. In all your ways acknowledge him, and he will make straight your paths" (Proverbs 3:5–6).

So, what our society is conditioning us with—busyness, success, popularity, achievement, and the "sickness" of more and more and more"—can, in fact, be translated as a way of cutting down on our dependence on God when God wants us to depend on him. He is not impressed by human wisdom, worldly influence, the strong, the rich, or the powerful. God's criteria are different. God delights in using people who appear to be the "least" of his children and whose childlike humility makes them seem ordinary and often overlooked by everyone else. And yet these children of God receive the supernatural power to do great things. Consider what St. Paul wrote:

> Consider your own call, brothers and sisters: not many of you were wise by human standards, not many were powerful, not many were of noble birth. But God chose what is foolish in the world to shame the wise; God chose what is weak in the world to shame the strong; God chose what is low and despised in the world, things that are not, to reduce to nothing things that are, so that no one might boast in the presence of God. He is the source of your life in Christ Jesus, who became for us wisdom from God, and righteousness and sanctification and redemption, in order that, as it is written, "Let the one who boasts, boast in the Lord." (1 Corinthians 1:26–30)

God's true people understand that the key to effectiveness is not their impressive resume but God's presence in them. This is why they are humble. They understand that they are neither in control nor the exception. They are simply, like anyone else, part of the human race. They can trust God because they do not have an inflated sense of their existence and self-worth. They know that their real worth comes from their creator and not from having their names printed in the headlines of the day. They just listen to God. They hear him. They obey him. They constantly check with him on the directions they are taking. They let go and surrender control, for they know that as long as they are in control, God wouldn't be. They learn to receive everything from God. They stand like the "tax collector" (see Luke 18:9–14)) not in the realm of "right and righteousness" but in the realm of mercy. This is where they meet God and find their salvation.

"The desperate need today," observed Richard Foster, "is not for a greater number of intelligent people or gifted people but for deep people." In so many ways we seem to be modernists in our hearts, minds, and lifestyles. Not only are we entertained by celebrities, trivial pursuits, and consumer products, but we are convinced that the latest is the best, that respect stems from conformity to mainstream "values," and that progress consists in jumping to, and embracing, "what is next" as if the grass is greener "over there"—in another church, another marriage, another house, another job. But, sooner or later, we cannot but see how shallow all these things are by themselves, and we turn our eyes to what gives them the depth of meaning. We surrender to the Absolute. Deep people know their limits and accept the limitless of God. Their story is a love story with the Infinite "for in [God they] live and move and have [their] being" (Acts 17:28).

Total surrender should not be used, however, as an excuse for irresponsibility, recklessness, or passivity on our part. Quite the opposite, total surrender means obeying God's will and commandments and letting his Gospel and Holy Scripture guide our lives in all things—temporal and spiritual—down to the smallest details.

In total surrender there are no halfway measures. By requiring giving our all for the All, total surrender is, in fact, nothing less than total participation in God's plan for ourselves and for the world. Therefore, we have a lot to do for the task is immense.

It is when Brother Lawrence was prepared to lay down his life for God, that he felt the great freedom from the bonds of the self with all its worries, ambitions, and its limitless preoccupations. Indeed, nothing can give more freedom and joy than knowing, loving, and serving God. Our world would be the ideal world—the realized kingdom of God—if we often remind ourselves, as Brother Lawrence said, "that our only concern in this life is to please God and that everything else is folly and vanity" (*Presence*, 67).

Pause. Ponder St. Alphonsus de Ligouri's line: "We cannot offer God anything more pleasing than to say: Take us, Lord, we give thee our entire will. Only let us know thy will and we will carry it out."

Personal Considerations

1. What is your definition of prayer? What prayers do you say with words? What prayers have you experienced without words?

   _____

   _____

   _____

   _____

2. Brother Lawrence did not see a difference between fixed times for prayer and any other times. If what he believes is true, what then would be the role of "religious things" in our lives, whch are made in particular times and places? Is it easier for you to see God in "religious things" rather than in everyday things? Explain.

   _____

   _____

_____

_____

3. How does the presence of God in all things that include the "ordinary" and the "secular" change the way we perceive them? How would you define the words "sacred" and "profane," "religious" and "secular," and "spiritual" and "mundane" anyway? What difference does your perception of them make in the way you live your life? Today, in every act that you do, consciously try to see the sacred. Explain how you have transformed or how you can transform all your daily activities into sacred actions, made in the presence of God.

_____

_____

_____

_____

4. After a day in the presence of God, please list the changes you have observed in your life.

_____

_____

_____

_____

Affirmation: *God is my origin, my destination, and Jesus is my companion and guide for the journey.*

Now, create a relevant affirmation of your own based on your experience and/or the above personal considerations.

Closing Prayer

O God, you are the source of everything and the designer of every structure of our life.

You did not create us to be lifeless, useless, and formless.

You have given us hands, mind, and heart to be your hands, mind, and heart in this process world.

You have made us recipients of your grace, instruments of your will, and executors of your plan.

Grant us the gift of discernment so we can see your divine will in our life and never fall from the grace of your presence.

O God, dear God, be the very center of our life. Be totally involved with all our decisions and actions. Share all the details of our ordinary life.

And, dear God,

Today I totally surrender my life to you for I know that true life is a God-job. By myself, I can neither change myself, nor I can change anybody else, and not even anything else.

Take my fear, doubt, worry, anxiety, pretense, and the desire to be in control, and work on me.

Take my pain, suffering, rejection, sadness, and grief.

Take my struggles, hard work, and my sense of duty and
responsibility, too.

Take the dichotomy of my mind, the paradox of my heart,
my dreams, and my ever-growing longing.

Prune me. Make adjustments. Be involved in every detail
of my life. Be more in me so I can be less of me. No one
can do it better than you, dear Lord. This is really hard;
it's a God-job.

Be me so I can be you. Amen!

Now, write your own personalized closing prayer for today
based on "God's involvement with you and your involvement
with God."

Day Five

Practicing the Presence of God: A Way of Life

Do you live in the presence of God at all times?

Invitation to presence: As believers, we live in the presence and great joy of our faithful God.

Focus: Continual conversation with God.

Opening Prayer: Lord, I often feel perplexed and distressed when I experience life's circumstances. Please help me to believe that you are in charge. Grant me the grace to better understand that you know me perfectly, that you call me by name, and that you love me.

Scripture Reading

Pray without ceasing. (1 Thessalonians 5:17)

Whether you eat or drink, or whatever you do, do everything for the glory of God. (1 Corinthians 10:31)

Do not be conformed to this world, but be transformed by the renewing of your minds, so that you may discern what is the will of God—what is good and acceptable and perfect. (Romans 12:2)

Learning from Brother Lawrence

We do not always have to be in church to be with God. We can make of our hearts an oratory where we can withdraw from time to time to converse with him there, gently, humbly, and lovingly. Everyone is capable of these familiar conversations with God, some more, some less. He knows what we can do. (*Presence*, 69)

> "We do not always have to be in church to be with God. We can make of our hearts an oratory where we can withdraw from time to time to converse with him there gently, humbly and lovingly."
>
> —*Presence*, 69

Neither fitness nor learning is required to approach God, only a heart resolved to devote itself exclusively to him, and to love him alone. (*Presence*, 96)

Remember, I beg you, what I recommended to you, that is, to think of God often, night and day, in all your activities, and even when you relax. He is always near you and with you; do not leave him alone. You would consider it rude to leave a friend who is visiting you by himself; then why abandon God and leave him alone? Do not forget him. Think of him often, adore him continually, live and die with him. This is the true occupation of a Christian; in a word, this is our trade. If we don't know it, we must learn it! (*Presence*, 71)

Reflection

God's will for us is to engage in continual conversation with him; walk with him in faith, love, and simplicity; and let him be involved totally in all that we think, say, and do. This is in essence what can be called the holy habit of the practice of the presence of God.

The practice of the presence of God should not be understood as an aspect or a compartment of a divided life; it is rather a life that is whole, integrated, unified, and centered on God. It is a way of life. Also, as Brother Lawrence believes, it is available to anyone, at any time, and in any circumstance.

When we live a life of quiet joy, no matter what our circumstances are; when we feel content, no matter how big or small our gifts are; and when we radiate peace, love, and joy, no matter how harsh aggravations seem to overcome us we know that we are practicing the holy habit of the practice of the presence of God.

In times of joy or pain, prosperity or poverty, good health or illness, ups or downs of life, we should always remember the essentials of the practice of the presence of God, which are engaging in continual conversation with God; walking with God in love, humility, simplicity, and faith; and thinking nothing and doing nothing that may displease him.

Understood this way, the practice of the presence of God is an ever-present reality that serves as a reference to return to every time we feel that something is out of balance in our lives and to make the necessary correction to conform with God's will. Jesus' message for us was his way of living—thinking, saying, and doing—according to the Father's will. Is the presence of God easy to practice? No, it is not. Brother Lawrence is the first to admit it. He said:

> I know that, to reach this state, the first steps are very difficult, and that we must act purely in faith. Furthermore, we

know we can do anything with God's grace, and he never refuses it to those who earnestly ask him for it. Knock at his door, keep knocking, and I tell you that he will open to you in his time if you do not give up, and that he will give you, all at once, what he held of giving for years. (*Presence*, 81)

He also said: "You don't become a saint in a day" (*Presence*, 67).

Indeed, let us not pretend that keeping in touch with God throughout the day is something easy. We have all experienced repeated frustration, disappointments, and failures in attempting it. We've all experienced the necessity of a major and painful period of adjustment to God's will, and often a harder time to discern God's will in the first place. Also, despite the best intentions we may have, our past experiences, old habits, and the conditioning of our usual familiar circles of expectations, misconceptions, superstitions, and selfishness try to force us to get ahead of God or to think that God does not know how to handle our own affairs as we do ourselves. The practice of the presence of God helps us to move in God's time and way. Also, the art of moving in God's time and way consolidates the practice of the presence of God.

Brother Lawrence chose to do everything he did for the love of God, and he "renounced for His love everything that was not Himself," and then he added, "I began to live as if only he and I existed in the world" (*Presence*, 75). Consequently, whatever he did, he did it for God and with God. Together, they cooked. Together, they ran errands. Together, they scrubbed pots. Together, they suffered. Together, they had joy. Therefore, everything acquired great value.

To be conscious of God's presence in our lives, moment by moment, is the key to living a Christian life in the midst of the busyness of everyday life. This is also how we establish a personal relationship with God and how we spiritually grow in his presence. Here are some suggestions to help us do that:

1. *Begin the day with God in your mind and heart.* Let God be first. Focus on him by worshipping him. Meditate on a hymn or a psalm. Thank God for a new morning and ask for the gift of a holy and blessed day. The psalmist said: "O Lord, in the morning you hear my voice; in the morning I plead my case to you, and watch" (Psalm 5:3). There is a lot of validity to what it has been often said: "The experts say how you spend the first hour of your day plays a major role in determining how the rest of your day will go."

> To be conscious of God's presence in our lives, moment by moment, is the key to living a Christian life in the midst of the busyness of everyday life.

2. *Pray.* Give yourself to God. Pray for your needs and the needs of others. God promised not to abandon us. Ask him for help. It is good to have a special time for prayer, but when we practice the presence of God, any time is a special time for prayer. Do not wait for formal times to pray. The whole of life can be prayer.

3. *Secure a private place and a regular time.* The place and time in which you choose to connect with God are not as important as just doing it, but initially to form the seed habit, you may need to rely on a particular sacred space and a particular sacred time you are sure you will never

miss. Then expand it to other places and times. Never say, "I don't have time." You know you do. You will have more time when you try to waste a little less of it. Never say, "This is not the right place." You know that God can be reached everywhere.

4. *Read a few lines from the Scripture.* Ponder Psalm 119 especially when it says: "I treasure your word in my heart, so that I may not sin against you" (v. 11), and "the unfolding of your words gives light; it imparts understanding to the simple" (v. 130).

5. *Love solitude and silence.* Make time throughout your busy day to spend a few moments alone with God in silence. "God is the friend of silence," said Mother Teresa of Calcutta. We should be silent in order to grasp the truth of what Psalm 46 says, "Be still, and know that I am God!" (v. 10). Indeed, God speaks to the quiet and attentive heart. As much as possible, we should stay away from time-wasters and time-robbers such as gossip and too much telephone talk and television watching. We should learn to be silent and listen. Listen to silence. Real silence is presence. In this contemplative silence, God whispers to the heart.

6. *Keep God at the center.* We should keep God at the center of our lives so that we can see him in our daily routines and events, do nothing that he doesn't do first, and then do nothing that may displease him.

7. *Be thankful.* Don't ever take anything for granted. Be thankful to God—the giver of all that you are and have—every moment of your life. "Give thanks in all circumstances," wrote St. Paul in his first letter to the Thessalonians (5:18),

and let the Lord direct your day because "We know that all things work together for good for those who love God, who are called according to his purpose" (Romans 8:28). Live always with an attitude of gratitude.

8. *Acknowledge God's presence by taking time to rejoice in the Lord in every situation.* We should "Rejoice in the Lord always" (Philippians 4:4). The psalmist said: "You show me the path of life. In your presence there is fullness of joy; in your right hand are pleasures forevermore" (Psalm 16:11).

9. *Share the faith with others.* Sharing the faith with others is another way to be in the presence of God. Fellowship with other believers and witnessing to believers and nonbelievers can certainly mark in obvious ways God's presence. Experience and tradition show that belonging to a community where the love of God is truly lived and expressed is an essential aspect of practicing the presence of God. We can even say that the presence of God is most authentic when it is lived in community.

10. *Radiate God's presence.* At work, say to yourself that you are working for God. Send divine love to everyone you meet. Give them a smile and the encouragement they need. See God working in you and in them. When they are uplifted, they become friendly, and you will feel the same, and even more. God's presence transforms everything.

> God's presence transforms everything.

11. *Do what you do for the love of God.* Mother Teresa of Calcutta said it best: "We can do not great things—only small things with great love."

12. *Practice, practice, practice.* The "don't quit," "keep going and trying," and "persist and persevere" recommendations make the difference. When we want to "get good at" something, we practice. Unless for misfortunes or inappropriate methods, the result of persistence is attainment. Even though changing habits, routines, and patterns may be difficult, if we want to do something we just choose other habits, routines, and patterns and keep practicing until they become part of us. We know that God chose to be in our lives. We should choose to meet God there and practice his presence so that we can say with St. Paul: "It is no longer I who live, but it is Christ who lives in me" (Galatians 2:20).

The blessed life is the daily walk with God. Growing in such a relationship is the path to real life.

Pause: Ponder St. Catherine of Siena's thought, "Then the soul is in God and God in the soul, just as the fish in the sea and the sea in the fish."

Personal Considerations

1. Below write about a person you know or have read about who is living or has lived in the presence of God as a way of life. What have you learned, or emulated, from this person?

_____

_____

_____

_____

2. What aspects of our culture seem to distract you from the presence of God in your life? How aware are you of the presence of God in your life, in the life of others, and in the universe? Explain how your life as lived now reflects—or does not reflect—the presence of God. What changes can you make to realize God's presence your life?

_____

_____

_____

_____

3. Visualize your life a year from today. How will your life be different if God's presence is in your everyday activities and relationships? Explain in detail.

_____

_____

_____

_____

Affirmation: *In any circumstance of my life, I turn my eyes and heart to God.*

Now, create a relevant affirmation of your own based on your experience and/or the above personal considerations.

Closing Prayer

If I am created in your image, O God who is love by
definition, I must then be from love, of love, for love.

Today I want to be worthy of this love, which is the only
response you want from me.

Today and ever after I want to love you, as you commanded, with all my heart and all my soul and all my
mind and all my strength. Please enable me to do so.

Teach me to love you in every person I encounter. Direct
my steps in your service in every need I meet. Let my
heart praise you in all of creation. Let nothing prevent
or distract me from being in your loving presence—
neither good health nor sickness, neither fame nor ano-
nymity, neither power nor weakness, neither wealth
nor poverty, and neither favorable events nor bad luck.

Loving God, help me to always choose to be the person
you want me to be—in your image of love.

Today I will love your creations.

Today I will love myself, and my neighbor as myself.

Today I open doors, windows, and even roofs for those
who need to be in your presence, be healed by you, and
journey with you.

Today I will immensely enjoy the greatest of your gifts—
your presence in the universe

Today let your will be made manifest in me and through me.

Today let your presence prevail on earth. Amen!

Now, write your own closing prayer for today based on
"Practicing the Presence of God: A Way of Life."

Day Six

Growing in Gratitude

Are you thankful for all God's gifts?

Invitation to presence: My awareness of the presence of God in my life makes me thankful for blessings large and small, for the expected and the unexpected, and for every special person and event in my life.

Focus: Gratitude for everything.

Opening Prayer: Thank you, God, for blessing me with your presence, in me and around me. Please guide me onto the pathways of blessing others with your blessings.

Scripture Reading

At that time Jesus said, "I thank you, Father, Lord of heaven and earth, because you have hidden these things from the wise and the intelligent and have revealed them to infants. (Matthew 11:25; Luke 10:21; see also John 11:41)

Thanks be to God for his indescribable gift! (2 Corinthians 9:15)

Give thanks in all circumstances. (1 Thessalonians 5:18)

Learning from Brother Lawrence

Join me in thanking him, please, for his great goodness to
me, for I cannot esteem highly enough the great number
of graces he bestows on me, a miserable sinner. May he be
blessed by all, Amen. (*Presence*, 76)

Our God is infinitely good and knows what we need. I
have always known he would bring you low. He will come
to raise you up in his own time, and when you least expect
it. Hope in him more than ever. Join me in thanking him
for the graces he gives you, especially for the strength and
patience he gives you in your afflictions. This is an obvious sign of his care for you. Find consolation in him and
thank him for everything. (*Presence*, 63)

We can continue our loving exchange with him, remain-
ing in his holy presence sometimes by an act of adora-
tion, praise, or desire, other times by acts of oblation,
thanksgiving, or anything else that our minds can devise.
(*Presence*, 59–60)

Reflection

Gratitude comes easily when we have good health, prosperity, and joy, but it seems very difficult and even unthinkable in
times of illness, trouble, and sadness. In both cases and because
it draws from the deep well of the soul, gratitude has the power
to help us always meet our needs, especially in times of scar-
city, darkness, and confusion. Gratitude is a realization of the
gift of life, a shift toward what we really are and what we have
been given, and a statement of gracious contentment.

A grateful person sees new possibilities where an ungrateful person sees only problems. A grateful person sees little miracles everywhere, where an ungrateful person sees only obstacles and impossibilities. A grateful person thanks God for what he or she has, where an ungrateful person complains about what he or she does not have. A grateful person uses his or her talents, where an ungrateful person envies others' talents. A grateful person sees in others—any others—the work of God, where the ungrateful person sees in them a reason for adversity and distress.

> A grateful person sees new possibilities where an ungrateful person sees only problems.

True, you can see the cup half empty if you want and focus on what is lacking in your life. You can go complaining about your fate, your family situation, your pocketbook, and the lack of sensitivity of others. Many people do just that. But you can also see the cup half full and focus on the abundant blessings you have and you take for granted and on every good thing that is on its way to you. Actually, it is in the laws of life that being grateful for what we already have attracts extra good to us. Gratitude is like a magnet that draws to us more friends, health, love, peace, and more spiritual and material good. Gratitude has the power to transform melancholy into cheerfulness, to lift depression into the light of God, and to give the wings of faith to a dispirited life. Gratitude can turn a meal into a party, a house into a home, a foe into a friend, and a routine into a celebration. Gratitude gives birth to other virtues; Cicero remarked, "Gratitude is not only the greatest virtue, but the

> "Gratitude is not only the greatest virtue, but the parent of all others."
>
> —*Cicero*

parent of all others." Gratitude allows us to see life, and live it, differently. For Albert Einstein, "There are only two ways to live your life. One is as though nothing is a miracle. The other is as though everything is a miracle." Gratitude lets us see life as a miracle.

Even in times of troubles and adversities, after some initial painful responses, our eyes and hearts can gradually see the miracle of life through faith. Sometimes a crisis can open our eyes to the gift and value of life more than anything else can. In spite of its dark side, a misfortune of a sort can give us a fresh outlook on the world we never had before, and we start to appreciate every minute we are alive. It can awaken us to being aware of the obvious—God's overwhelming graciousness to us. When we are awake to the "All is a gift from God," we want to gratefully stay awake to this palpable truth. For Henri Nouwen, "pruning"—suffering, pain, or misfortune—is not punishment but purification that can bring us closer to God. He beautifully wrote:

> Pruning means cutting, reshaping, removing what diminishes vitality. When we look at a pruned vineyard, we can hardly believe it will bear fruit. But when harvest time comes we realize that the pruning enables the vine to concentrate its energy and produce more grapes than it could have had it remained unpruned. Grateful people are those who can celebrate even the pains of life because they trust that when harvest time comes the fruit will show that the pruning was not punishment but purification.

Gratitude acknowledges that all that we are and have was given to us out of love and should be celebrated with great joy, because everything that happens—good or bad—must eventually turn into a blessing, even though we may not realize it at the time, and only if our faith in God deepens. Don't we sometimes learn from a rocky road, with its twists and turns, ups and downs, and detours and diversions, more than we learn from a smooth, flowery, and easy path? Even, and especially, when things get rough, gratitude will help us turn our gaze to God's greater plan. A problem can sometimes be a blessing in disguise. St. Paul recommends to "[give] thanks to God the Father at all times and for everything in the name of our Lord Jesus Christ" (Ephesians 5:20). He sees the redemptive benefits of that "at all times and for everything" state of gratitude. With this, he points to one of the most sensitive tenets of our Christian existence.

At any time, we all have many things to be grateful for and thank God—the Source of all gifts—for them all and one by one.

We should prayerfully practice thanks-saying as well as thanks-doing. When we give thanks to God, we profess our conviction that everything we have is the expression of his love to us and we acknowledge his ongoing involvement in our lives. When we enjoy the talents he has granted us and carry out our mission he has assigned to us, we acknowledge our grateful awareness of the fact that whatever we were able to accomplish was the result of his generous grace and help. Wouldn't the best way to thank the giver be to enjoy the gift and use it? Thank God for his gifts and use them for his glory. God created you as unique; no one is like you. You

> At any time, we all have many things to be grateful for and thank God—the Source of all gifts—for them all and one by one.

have your own abilities, talents, and unlimited potential to the point where you can be like him. St. John wrote: "Beloved, we are God's children now; what we will be has not yet been revealed. What we do know is this . . . we will be like him" (1 John 3:2).

Please count your blessings every morning and thank God for them and for the new day ahead. Even though you may not know what will happen in that day, you do know, however, that God is within every situation you will face, every decision you will make, and every action you will take. G. K. Chesterton insightfully said:

> You say grace before meals. All right. But I say grace before the concert and the opera, and grace before the play and pantomime, and grace before I open a book, and grace before sketching, painting, swimming, fencing, boxing, walking, playing, dancing and grace before I dip the pen in the ink.

Thank God for the gifts of life and health, family and friends, food and daily work, wisdom and understanding, and the peace of mind and heart. Thank God for your problems and challenges; they allow you to grow in wisdom and compassion. An ancient proverb says, "A donkey may carry a heavy load of sandalwood on its back and never know its preciousness—only its weight." Aggravations, when overcome, and problems, when solved, make us stronger and wiser. Acknowledge that God has many doors, and he is at work in you and through you. So, giving thanks helps us, not only to go through, but to grow through. William Shakespeare summarized it best when he said, "I can no other answer make but thanks, and thanks, and ever thanks."

Giving thanks helps you to recharge your energy in mind, body, spirit, and daily activities. Small things will do it. Try some of them. Allow yourself to be surprised by whatever makes you catch your breath: a rainbow, the first snow of winter, the first buds of spring, a sunset, the smile of a baby, a beautiful song—savor the moment with wonder and admiration. Observe the way you can see, hear, smell, touch, taste, think, speak, walk, breathe, and eat. Watch a bird in flight. Look for formations of the clouds. Listen to your soul, heart, and mind. Write a poem. Laugh. Give a gift for no reason. Write a letter. Create something unique. Marvel at a flower. Enjoy a cup of tea.

Gaze into the heavens in a starry night. Feel the wind in your hair. Plant something and see it grow. Meditate on God's goodness. Inhale and exhale a deep prayer of thankfulness for all these and for many more.

Brother Lawrence was a simple lay Carmelite whose talents and skills were limited to the point that the only work he was assigned to was to be a cook and a sandal maker. In spite of these humble jobs and in spite of his suffering from poor health especially during the last years of his life, he realized how privileged he was for "the great outpouring of grace" on him. He wrote in his twelfth letter: "Join me in thanking him, please, for his great goodness to me, for I cannot esteem highly enough the great number of graces he bestows on me, a miserable sinner. May he be blessed by all. Amen." (*Presence*, 76).

No matter how down you are by feeling unappreciated, a grateful inventory for what you have will make you smile. No matter how fearful you are for lacking talents and skills to do what you want to do, gratitude will show you new possibilities. No matter how bitter and resentful you feel vis-à-vis past experiences, gratitude will make you transcend the hurts and open new paths before you.

Moreover, an attitude of gratitude, according to recent studies made at the University of California and at the University of Miami, has benefits on health, wholeness, and general well-being. The findings show that people who practice expressions of gratitude feel better about their lives as a whole; beside the fact that they have fewer states of stress, depression, and physical symptoms, they enjoy higher levels of the positive states of alertness, vitality, attentiveness, optimism, capacity to be empathic, determination, life satisfaction, and energy to achieve personal goals. If this is the case and if gratitude is the mark of an essentially healthy person, why in the world do some people find it so difficult to be thankful? It's because they tend to worship independence—we love to be able to say, "I am self-made, and I don't owe anyone anything." It's also because of a self-centered attitude—we love to be the measure of everything. Our culture immerses us in this kind of value, and we forget that the center of the universe is not our "self" but God.

A prayerful attitude of thankfulness is a powerful expression of practicing the presence of God. It is part of the continual conversation with him, the awareness of him, and the communion with him.

Gratitude is an expression of faith, love, hope, trust, humility, and simplicity. Indeed, all these virtues are included in the "Thank you, Father" the beautiful phrase that, when said consciously and repeatedly, has the power to transform the

> A prayerful attitude of thankfulness is a powerful expression of practicing the presence of God.

person and his or her environment at all levels and for good, making us a truly "new creation" (Galatians 6:15).

"Thank you, Father," which is the sign that we are doing his will, certainly brings happy and holy results. God wants to shape us in his image. He wants to reveal himself through us; we then start to understand our higher purpose and praise him in us. "Thank you, Father" should be our ultimate prayer. Indeed, as Meister Eckhart said, "If the only prayer you ever say in your entire life is thank you, it will be enough."

Let us thank God for the gift of life and not take life for granted. Let us be unceasingly grateful for the extraordinary gift of self-worth—we are God's children. Let us grow in gratitude and delight in God's wonders with a joyful heart.

Pause: Ponder David Steindl-Rast's thought, "Suddenly everything is simple. We can drop all the big, cumbersome terms. Gratefulness says it all."

Personal considerations

1. Write about an especially difficult time in your life. What were your feelings of that time? What have you learned about life from this experience? How has your faith deepened from this experience?

_____

_____

_____

_____

2. Think about your current obstacles of disappointments in life. How could you turn each one of them into a blessing and say, "Thank you, Father!"?

_____

_____

_____

_____

3 List everything you are grateful for in your life. Count your blessings one by one. After each one say, "Thank you, Father!" How can you share more of your gifts from God with others?

_____

_____

_____

_____

Affirmation. *God is the source of my life. My thoughts and actions are expressions of gratitude for his illimitable blessings.*

Now, create a relevant affirmation of your own based on your experience and/or the above personal considerations.

Closing prayer

"Thank you, Father" for all you have given me.

Thank you for my soul, heart, mind, and body.

Thank you for the ability to see, smell, touch, hear, and taste.

Thank you for the day and night, time and space, and yesterday, today, and tomorrow.

Thank you for family and friends, bosses and coworkers, and citizens and foreigners.

Thank you for the ability to walk, talk, and work.

Thank you for inspiring me to think, speak, act, and pray.

Thank your for the ability to grow, change, and transform myself and my world.

Thank you for the freedom to be who I really am and will be.

Thank you for the opportunity to imagine what could be if I truly live in your presence.

Thank you for the grace that helps me to live in your presence.

Thank you for your infinite love that is still a mystery to me.

Thank you for making me your child—the expression of your divine love.

Thank you for being to me closer than my skin, closer than my eyes, and closer than my thoughts and self.

Thank you for giving me the privilege to have access
to you at any time and without any prior notice.
I acknowledge that I can do more with you than I can
do with my limited capacity. I am grateful that when
I can't, you can, and that there is nothing that together
we cannot do—all is your grace.

I am grateful that, with you, my dear Lord, I don't have to
hide my failures and my needs for you always meet me
where I am.

And please, Father, help me to be aware of your blessings
and to always be able to say, "Thank you, Father" at
any moment of my life. Help me to transform my life
into thanksliving. Amen!

Now, write your own personalized closing prayer for today
based on "Growing in Gratitude."

Day Seven

Living the Meaningful Life

Are you living God's life?

Invitation to presence: Centered in the presence of God, I feel serene, secure, and revitalized because everything in my life falls into place.

Focus: Living God's life.

Opening Prayer: Without you, O God, I cannot do anything, but with you I can do everything. You are the Lord of the future. You hold the future—my future, the future of my family and country, and the future of the world. I put all my hope in you. You are my future because you are in my present.

Scripture Reading

Abide in me as I abide in you. Just as the branch cannot bear fruit by itself unless it abides in the vine, neither can you unless you abide in me. I am the vine, you are the branches. Those who abide in me and I in them bear much fruit, because apart from me you can do nothing. (John 15:4–5)

If you continue in my word, you are truly my disciples; and you will know the truth, and the truth will make you free. (John 8:31–32)

I can do all things through him who strengthens me. (Philippians 4:13)

Learning from Brother Lawrence

The first benefit that the soul receives from the [practice of the] presence of God is that its faith becomes more intense and efficacious in all life's situations, and especially in times of need, since it easily obtains graces in moments of temptation and in the inevitable dealings with creatures. For the soul, accustomed to the practice of faith by this exercise, sees and senses God present in a simple remembrance. It calls out to him easily and effectively, thus obtaining what it needs. (*Presence*, 42)

This [practice of the] presence of God, somewhat difficult in the beginning, secretly accomplishes marvelous effects in the soul, draws abundant graces from the Lord, and, when practiced faithfully, imperceptibly leads it to this simple awareness, to this loving view of God present everywhere, which is the holiest, the surest, the easiest, and the most efficacious form of prayer. (*Presence*, 41)

This practice inspires the will with a scorn for creatures, and inflames it with a sacred fire of love. Since the will is always with God who is a consuming fire, this fire reduces to ashes all that is opposed to it. The soul thus inflamed can live only in the presence of tits God, a presence that produces in its heart a holy ardor, a sacred zeal and a strong desire to see this God loved, known, served, and adored by all creatures. (*Presence*, 42)

Reflection

To identify ourselves with what we do or possess is, physically, more noticeable than to identify ourselves with who we really are; "who" and "what" we are is invisible to the eyes. It seems more convenient to be "religious" than to love our neighbor. It is easier to go to church than to spend real time with God. But when we decide to spend real time with the Lord—hopefully unceasingly—we become more like him. We will see like he sees. We will think like he thinks. We will do things like he does.

What a difference this makes to us and to the world!

Indeed, when we practice the presence of God in our lives by having a continuous conversation with him—praying unceasingly—we begin to live his life in our daily activities. How could it be otherwise? Jesus said: "You will know them by their fruits. Are grapes gathered from thorns, or figs from thistles? In the same way, every good tree bears good fruit, but the bad tree bears bad fruit. A good tree cannot bear bad fruit, nor can a bad tree bear good fruit" (Matthew 7:16–18).

> When we practice the presence of God in our lives by having a continuous conversation with him— praying unceasingly— we begin to live his life in our daily activities.

The practice of the presence of God works!

Of course we are supposed to feed the hungry, shelter the homeless, oppose racial oppression, visit the sick, work for peace and justice, and help the dying. But "[we] are not social workers," as Mother Teresa of Calcutta said when she was talking about the Missionaries of Charity. "[We] are contemplatives in the midst of the world." Therefore, our work should be the fruit of prayer and practicing the presence of God in us and in others. This is why we will be able to do, as perfectly as we possibly can, anything for the love of God, and not for any other reason. St. Paul reminds us: "If I give away all my possessions, and if I hand over my body so I may boast, but do not have love, I gain nothing" (1 Corinthians 13:3). By loving others—whoever they are—and loving our work—whatever it is—we accomplish a life of ministry. Our relationship and our work will acquire a completely different quality. The presence of God is not like a lake to be enjoyed when we need a break. It is rather like a river whose water—the unconditional love of God—flows through us and into the lives of others and into all that we do. St. John wrote: "Beloved, since God loved us so much, we also ought to love one another. No one has ever seen God; if we love one another, God lives in us, and his love is perfected in us" (1 John 4:11–12).

Entering the presence of God does not depend on our worthiness. It is in our nature and it lies deep in our psyche, it seems, that we always want to prove that we own our salary, the respect of a spouse or friends, a place of honor in a community just to acquire a position of significance in our own eyes and in the eyes of others. For that purpose, we do everything possible such as schooling, training, experiencing, practicing, and looking for the right connections. We may have the right to do that. But this conduct does not apply to the presence of God. We do not earn the presence of God, for the presence of God depends on God's grace and mercy. God's nature is unconditional love and mercy. His love imparts worth to us. We acquire significance not because we did something great but because his infinite love gives us true worth, which we should learn to receive. It takes time to learn to receive it. It takes time to pray, meditate, study and ponder the Scripture, and especially to listen to God. The practice of the presence of God does just that.

Living in the presence of God not only brings us the comfort we need in times of crisis—suffering, fear, generalized gloom and malaise, and depression—it also changes our heart of stone into a heart of flesh, a heart that is vulnerable, compassionate, and empathetic. "I will give them one heart, and put a new spirit within them; I will remove the heart of stone from their flesh and give them a heart of flesh, so that they may follow my statutes and keep my ordinances and obey them. Then they should be my people, and I will be their God" (Ezekiel 11:19–20).

The practice of the presence of God produces in the soul wonderful effects, and as Brother Lawrence put it, "a holy ardor, a sacred zeal and a strong desire to see this God loved known, served, and adored by all creatures" (*Presence*, 42).

Inspired by the gift of the divine love that transfigures us, our soul blossoms forth for the entire world to see through every action we perform because, then, "our only concern in this life is to please God" (*Presence*, 67).

When we live in the "all for the All" and "the All in all" relationship, we are:

- blessed (see Matthew 5:1–11),
- comforted (see John 14:16–17),
- never alone (see Matthew 28:20; Hebrews 13:5),
- never afraid (see Psalm 23:4),
- never in panic (see Romans 8:28),
- never worried about clothing and food (see Luke 12:22–34),
- never worried about our weakness and how to pray (see Romans 8:26),

- never worried about problems or about what to say (see 1 Corinthians 10:13; Mark 13:11),
- never worried about God giving up on us (see Philippians 1:6),
- never worried about anything (see Philippians 4:6),
- kept away form sin (see Psalm 119:25; Isaiah 40:28–31),
- living in freedom (see 2 Corinthians 3:17),
- living in peace and joy (see Romans 14:17),
- rested (see Matthew 11:28–30),
- renewed and rejuvenated (see 2 Corinthians 5:17; Revelation 21:5; Psalm 104:30),
- capable of acquiring the divine life (see Galatians 2:20),
- powerful (see John 15:7; Luke 18:27; Philippians 4:13),
- aware of the source of all things (see Romans 11:36),
- conscious of the sacredness of all things and for doing all things for the glory of God (see 1 Corinthians 10:31),
- aware of being a temple of the Holy Spirit and aware of the things that are not of God (see 1 Corinthians 6:19),
- caring for others (see Matthew 25:40; 1 Thessalonians 5:11),
- loving (see Luke 6:20–38; 1 John 2:3–21; 4:20–21),
- provided with peace and rest (see 2 Chronicles 14:6; 15:15), and
- made the type of leader people want to follow (see 2 Chronicles 15:9).

Practicing the presence of God is like having a checking account. When we want to buy something, we just write a check, provided we have enough deposit in our account. Difficult times may arise in our lives, perplexing choices need to be dealt with, and tough decisions need to be made. If we do not have enough deposit in our spiritual account, we cannot properly face the challenges that confront us. Through practicing the presence of God and having continual conversation with him, we can be more assured of having

> Practicing the presence of God is not a matter of finding an hour a day to do it. It is rather a way of life—something that fits into our entire life.

enough to count on when needs arise. God is the reservoir that will never dry up and the deposit in our account will never be small and limited. Practicing the presence of God, therefore, is not a matter of finding an hour a day to do it. It is rather a way of life—something that fits into our entire life. And the more we do it, the easier it becomes. The easier it becomes, the better we will be in living and sharing Gospel truths and reaching our destiny.

A genuine practice of the presence of God will do for us what it did for Jesus. The same Spirit that led Jesus to the wilderness to pray, fast, reflect, and be tempted led him also into villages and towns to minister to the lonely and sinners, the sick and poor, and to the "righteous" and the "powerful" of this world. This same Spirit that leads us to a prayerful solitude and silence to reconsider our priorities and put our house in order will send us forth to the world that is waiting to be healed. We go back to the same family, same friends, same job, and same everything else. But somehow, they are the same no longer. God's presence initiates a relationship that cannot be broken. So say good-bye to familiar broken family bonds and friendships as well as to all the deceiving idols whose appeal and attraction can never be forever.

Nothing will stay the same when we see things with Christ's eyes. Whether he saw a child or a leper, a disciple or a prostitute, the joy of a wedding feast or the sorrow of the loss of a loved one, a friend or an executioner, Jesus always saw God. We too—everyone and not simply a few of us—can learn to see all that we are accustomed to see everyday, anywhere, anytime with Christ's eyes. And this is how, without other qualifications except our openness to God's movement in our lives through the practice of the presence of God, we bring our contribution to the "Thy kingdom come."

The purpose of your life is not to be lonely and empty, but to be "God's temple" (1 Corinthians 3:16). What is the use of a container without the contained, the cup without the beverage, the hearth without the fire, the ritual without the essence, the letter without the spirit, and the word without the meaning? We are created to be indwelt by the presence of God, which forms and shapes us, and through us reaches the entire world.

God's presence is not an abstract and ethereal concept. Quite the contrary, it is concrete and real. It defines your identity and shapes your destiny. If you can see yourself for what you are, God can see you also for what you can become. "For surely I know the plans I have for you, says the Lord, plans for your welfare and not for harm, to give you a future with hope. Then when you call upon me and come and pray to me, I will hear you" (Jeremiah 29:11–12). God's presence in you gives you clarity, enflames your life, and sets you in the right direction. It gives hope when facing the despair of distrust, deficit, defeat, disease, and death. It provides you with the answer to the

> God's presence in you gives you clarity, enflames your life, and sets you in the right direction.

question you should always ask yourself, "Is what I am doing in and with my life contributing to my eternity?"

God says, "You shall be holy, for I am holy" (Leviticus 11:45). This is the description of God's life, and this is how our life is supposed to be. In a practical way, we live God's life when we dedicate, consecrate, and let everything in life be shaped by his presence. This means that every aspect of our life should reflect what God would say and do and what carries his mark of morality, integrity, and excellence.

To the question, "Who am I?", you can answer by offering information taken from your resume or your health or work history. You can talk about your temperament, accomplishments, failures, position, family status, habits and attitudes, education, whom you are associated with, and everything you appear to be. Many people stop there. Please don't. Go deeper—much deeper; instead of identifying yourself with the way you are, identify yourself with the way God wants you to be.

The anthropological question, "Who am I?", the philosophical question, "Why am I here?", the sociological question, "How am I here?", and the theological question, "What God has to do with me?", cannot be separated. They are fundamentally interdependent. Therefore, we can never know ourselves unless we know God and we can never find fulfillment and happiness by seeking fulfillment and happiness but by seeking and finding God. Any identity that exists apart from its relationship to its source is simply a mirage.

In light of the presence of God in your soul, you will realize that, although distinct, you are not separate from God. When you connect the flow of your being to its Source, you will realize that your potential is unlimited. You are made in God's image. You are God's child. You are in union with God—the Reality. You may even want to say with the mystic St. Catherine of Genoa, "There is no me but God." In a sense, this is the most radical humility—"there is no me." But also, this is the peak of transformation—"but God." Then, you can say that the presence of God in you allowed you to discover that, only in God, you found your true identity and destiny, and only in God, you will experience the divine Self of infinite happiness, freedom, and peace.

Pause: Ponder this line from St. John of the Cross: "And here lies the remarkable delight of this awakening: the soul knows creatures through God and not God through creatures."

Personal Considerations

1. What areas of your life have lacked meaning up until recently? List significant changes you can make or have made to improve these areas of your life. Explain.

   _____

   _____

   _____

   _____

2. Write about a recent experience where you had difficulty seeing God in a person. Why did this occur? How can you alter this perception?

   _____

   _____

_____

_____

3. What have you learned about yourself as a result of practicing the presence of God? What kind of impact do you think that practicing the presence of God would have on this world?

_____

_____

_____

_____

Affirmation: *I best demonstrate God's existence in the world when I constantly live in his presence.*

Now, create a relevant affirmation of your own based on your experience and/or the above personal considerations.

Closing Prayer

Your Son, O God, is "the same yesterday and today and forever" (Hebrews 13:8). He is your facet and I want to see him again and again in every aspect of my life.

Help me to see him in the blue sky, the green mountain, and the blooming flowers.

Help me to see him in the lonely, the distressed, the ill, the outcast, the broken, and the abused.

Help me to see him in the events and circumstances that occur.

Help me to live in total presence of you as you are totally present in the here and now.

Help me to make of my prayer a life-giving relationship and not only a religious practice.

Help me to have the right perception of you. Let my theology—the way I see you—lead my anthropology— the way I see my fellow human beings, and let the way I see them in you and through you lead my understanding and practice of sociology and social order.

Help me to be a new person, and a new world will emerge because you "[make] all things new" (Revelation 21:5).

God, my God, you are a now-God; everything is present to you.

Help me to live your life.

Help me to be your presence to the world. Amen!

Now, write your own personalized closing prayer for today based on "Living a Meaningful Life."

Suggestions for Practicing the Presence of God

Take home with you the following suggestions; they can help you develop a personal rule to make the presence of God so natural that it becomes part of you (see *Presence*, 39–40):

1. Think, say, and do nothing that could displease God. Remind yourself that the only business in life is to please God. Think God at all times.

2. Convince yourself that your prayer time is not different from other times because God wants to be present in every area of your life.

3. Put your entire trust in God and never lose sight of him. Always put God first in everything, every day of your life.

4. Let God be your only Master by emptying your mind and heart of all other things.

5. Make of your faith in God the foundation for your actions and reactions.

6. Create a sacred place in the house or elsewhere where you can retire from to time to time to converse with God.

7. Repeat little acts of worships throughout the day such as "Lord, I am entirely yours," "God, I love you," "God, your will be done not mine."

8. Always look to God before, during, and after performing your usual duties.

9. "It is the Creator who teaches the truth" (*Presence*, 41) so open your heart to what he says and pay little attention to what others say.

10. Always remember that you are in divine company.

11. See God in those you live with, work with, worship with, and hang around with.

12. See your daily work as a Christian ministry.

13. Treat animals and things with care and reverence, as they are God's creations.

14. Even if it can be difficult to practice the presence of God at the beginning, never give up. Practice, practice, practice until it becomes a part of your nature.

15. Get help from God. With God, everything is possible. Never insult God by thinking that he cannot use you. God wants you to start over, again and again; he delights in new beginnings.

The Institute of Carmelite Studies promotes research and publication in the field of Carmelite spirituality. Its members are Discalced Carmelites, part of a Roman Catholic community — friars, nuns, and laity — who are heirs to the teaching and way of life of Teresa of Jesus and John of the Cross, men and women dedicated to contemplation and to ministry in the Church and the world. Information concerning their way of life is available through local diocesan Vocation Offices or from the Vocation Directors' Offices:

1233 S. 45th Street, Milwaukee, WI 53214

1 Fallons Lane 1628 London, ON, Canada N6A 4C1

P.O. Box 3420, San Jose, CA 95156-3420

5151 Marylake Drive, Little Rock, AR 72206